The Next Tech Wave

How Today's Gadgets Will Shape Tomorrow's World

Elise Harrington

TABLE OF CONTENT

Introduction

The world around us is changing at a pace we've never seen before. What once seemed like distant dreams, hovering cars, AI-driven homes, and gadgets that can think for us, are quickly becoming realities. We're on the cusp of a technological revolution that's reshaping every facet of our lives. From the devices we use to the way we live, work, and interact, technology is evolving so rapidly that what we considered "cutting-edge" a few years ago now seems outdated. This wave of innovation isn't just transforming gadgets; it's reshaping entire industries, altering societies, and opening up possibilities that once felt impossible.

Today, gadgets and AI systems have become so integrated into our lives that it's hard to imagine a world without them. Phones that know our habits, cameras that adjust themselves based on our surroundings, and smart homes that anticipate our needs, these aren't just novelties; they're building blocks for the future. Devices powered by artificial intelligence are not merely responding to our commands; they're learning from our actions, anticipating what we want, and often acting before we even think to ask. This seamless integration of AI, paired with gadgets that are smarter, faster, and more efficient, is changing how we live in profound ways.

But it's not just about today's tech; it's about what this tech is paving the way for tomorrow. Innovations we see today, like foldable OLED screens, AI-driven smart glasses, and ultra-portable projectors, are just the beginning. These advancements are forming the foundation for the next generation of technology. They're setting the stage for what's to come, creating a world where technology isn't just something we use, it's something that becomes a part of who we are.

Now is the perfect moment to take a closer look at this transformation. As we dive into the gadgets, devices, and systems that are leading this revolution, we'll explore how they're not only influencing the world around us but also laying the groundwork for a future we could once only dream of. The impact of these innovations is far-reaching, and we are standing at the edge of a new era, one defined by the tech of today, shaping the world of tomorrow.

Chapter 1: The Evolution of Gadgets

A Brief History of Personal Tech Gadgets

The journey of personal tech gadgets began in the mid-20th century, when the idea of portable, user-centric technology was more a dream than reality. The first major milestone was the creation of the computer. Early models, like the ENIAC in the 1940s, were massive, occupying entire rooms and requiring specialized knowledge to operate. These machines, while revolutionary, were not something the average person could use at home.

However, by the 1970s, things began to change. The advent of microprocessors paved the way for the development of personal computers. In 1975, the Altair 8800, often considered the first personal computer, was introduced. Although it lacked the user-friendly design of today's systems, it signaled a shift toward making computing accessible to the masses. This was a time when tech enthusiasts were building their own machines, and the idea of personal computing was taking root.

The 1980s saw the emergence of companies like Apple and IBM, bringing the personal computer into homes and offices. The IBM PC, released in 1981, and the Apple Macintosh, launched in 1984, were pivotal in making personal computing more accessible. These systems were still bulky but represented significant progress in the usability and affordability of computers. The Macintosh, in particular, revolutionized design with its graphical user interface (GUI), which replaced the cumbersome text-based interfaces that had dominated computing until then.

Fast forward to the 1990s and 2000s, and personal tech gadgets began to shrink in size while expanding in functionality. The laptop computer emerged, offering portability without sacrificing power, and the smartphone revolutionized communication. The first smartphones, like the Nokia 7110, introduced in 1999, were a far cry from today's multi-functional devices. They could make calls, send texts, and access the internet in a limited capacity, but it wasn't until the launch of the iPhone in 2007 that the smartphone became the powerhouse it is today. The iPhone brought together a phone, music player, web browser, and camera into one sleek, portable device.

Since then, gadgets have continued to evolve, with newer devices incorporating more advanced technology. Wearable tech, like the Apple Watch, and virtual assistants, such as Amazon's Alexa, have extended the functionality of smartphones and computers, making them more integrated into our everyday lives.

How Gadgets Have Revolutionized Everyday Life

The integration of smart devices into daily routines has fundamentally altered how we live, work, and communicate. One of the most significant changes has been in the way we interact with technology. No longer do we have to sit at a desk to use a computer; today, technology is mobile, allowing us to work, play, and socialize wherever we are. Smartphones, tablets, and laptops allow us to remain connected and productive whether we're at home, in transit, or at work.

One of the most obvious ways gadgets have revolutionized life is in the workplace. Today, many people can work remotely thanks to devices that allow for easy communication, collaboration, and access to information. Cloud computing and the rise of tools like Slack, Zoom, and Google Drive have made remote work seamless, even during times of global crises like the COVID-19 pandemic. The transition from traditional office spaces to virtual environments has been enabled by these gadgets, forever altering how businesses operate and how we view work-life balance.

In our personal lives, gadgets have transformed leisure activities. Streaming services like Netflix, Spotify, and YouTube have become central to how we consume entertainment, with devices like smart TVs and portable tablets making it easy to watch movies, listen to music, and enjoy video games from the comfort of our couches or on the go. Gaming consoles and personal computers are no longer just about playing games, they're social hubs, allowing us to connect with friends and strangers from all over the world. Virtual reality (VR) and augmented reality (AR) have further pushed the boundaries of gaming, offering immersive experiences that were once confined to science fiction.

Communication, too, has been forever changed. In the past, sending a letter or making a long-distance phone call were the primary ways people kept in touch. Today, social media, instant messaging, and video calls have made communication instantaneous. Smartphones allow us to send text messages, share photos and videos, and even conduct video conferences with people on the other side of the world, all at the touch of a button. Gadgets like smartwatches have added another layer, enabling users to communicate even more seamlessly without having to pull out their phones.

Even in the realm of health and wellness, gadgets have become essential. Fitness trackers like the Fitbit and Apple Watch help users monitor their physical activity, heart rate, and sleep patterns, making it easier to live healthier lives. These devices sync with mobile apps, giving users access to real-time data that can be used to improve their fitness routines and overall well-being. Additionally, smart home devices such as thermostats, lights, and security cameras are enhancing convenience and security, making it easier for people to control their environments.

Today's gadgets, powered by artificial intelligence (AI) and the Internet of Things (IoT), are even beginning to anticipate our needs, offering predictive functionality that makes daily tasks easier and more efficient. For example, voice assistants like Amazon's Alexa and Apple's Siri can perform tasks such as setting reminders, controlling the lights, or answering questions without needing manual input. This type of automation is not only convenient but also a glimpse into a future where gadgets work together to create smarter, more efficient living spaces.

In conclusion, gadgets have revolutionized everyday life by becoming integral to the way we work, play, and communicate. As technology continues to advance, we can expect these devices to become even more embedded in our daily routines, creating an ever-more connected and efficient world. The next wave of gadgets is sure to bring even more exciting innovations, making life more convenient, more interactive, and more enjoyable than ever before.

Chapter 2: Gadgets That Are Shaping Tomorrow

Wearable Technology: The Rise of Convenience

Wearable technology has quickly become one of the most exciting frontiers in personal tech, with devices that not only make our lives more convenient but also more interconnected. The future of wearables is defined by devices that offer seamless integration into our daily routines, elevating how we interact with the world around us. This section highlights two groundbreaking innovations that are helping shape the future of wearable tech: the Mudra Wristband and the RayNeo Air 3S.

The Mudra Wristband is a revolutionary device that allows users to control various devices through hand gestures. Unlike other wearables that rely on touchscreens or buttons, the Mudra Wristband interprets neural signals from the user's hand, enabling intuitive, gesture-based control. This wearable works by reading the electrical signals generated by the user's hand muscles and translating them into commands for electronic devices. It's an example of how AI and neural interfaces are merging to create a more natural, efficient way of interacting with technology.

One of the most remarkable aspects of the Mudra Wristband is its versatility. It can be paired with a variety of devices, from smartphones and smart TVs to music players, providing a hands-free way to control gadgets. Imagine changing the volume of your music or swiping through apps with just a flick of your wrist or the motion of your fingers. This device not only enhances convenience but also provides a new way to engage with technology that feels organic and effortless.

Moving from the wrist to the eyes, the RayNeo Air 3S AR glasses represent a bold step forward in the realm of augmented reality. These lightweight, stylish glasses offer users an immersive 201-inch virtual screen, ideal for gaming, watching movies, or even working. The RayNeo Air 3S provides a visual experience akin to having a massive screen right in front of you, without the need for a bulky headset or projector.

What sets these glasses apart is their 120Hz refresh rate, ensuring smooth, lag-free interactions for users engaged in gaming or media consumption. The ability to connect the glasses to your smartphone allows you to mirror content and apps directly to the display. The glasses are also designed for comfort, allowing users to wear them for extended periods without discomfort. Whether you're playing an AR game, watching your favorite TV show, or working on a presentation, the RayNeo Air 3S opens up endless possibilities for mobile entertainment and productivity.

As wearable technology continues to evolve, devices like the Mudra Wristband and RayNeo Air 3S are pushing the boundaries of how we engage with digital environments. These innovations offer a glimpse into a future where technology becomes a seamless extension of our senses, responding to natural movements and actions, enhancing both convenience and immersion in our daily lives.

Smart Home Devices: The Future of Home Automation

Smart home devices are another cornerstone of the tech revolution, shaping the future of how we live and interact with our living spaces. These devices are transforming homes into intelligent, efficient environments that respond to our needs and routines. The growing popularity of AI-powered systems and voice assistants has taken home automation to new heights, making it easier than ever to manage everything from lighting to security. Among the most intriguing innovations in this space are devices like the Irvine AI-powered Doorbell and the Flick Duo Smart Button.

The Irvine AI-powered Doorbell is a prime example of how AI is being used to enhance security and convenience in the home. This smart doorbell is equipped with a high-definition camera, facial recognition software, and AI algorithms that can identify visitors and alert homeowners when someone is at the door. What sets the Irvine doorbell apart is its ability to learn and adapt over time. The more it interacts with the homeowner, the better it becomes at recognizing familiar faces, distinguishing between family members and strangers, and even detecting unusual behavior.

In addition to its security features, the Irvine doorbell is also highly customizable. It can integrate with other smart devices in your home, like smart locks or lighting systems, allowing you to control access and respond to visitors remotely via a smartphone app. This kind of automation is just the beginning of how AI and machine learning are redefining home security, making it smarter, safer, and more intuitive.

Equally transformative is the Flick Duo Smart Button, a simple yet powerful tool that adds a layer of convenience to any smart home setup. The Flick Duo is a minimalist, easy-to-install button that can be programmed to control various smart devices, from lights and thermostats to music systems and security cameras. What makes the Flick Duo unique is its simplicity and versatility. With just two buttons, users can trigger multiple actions based on their needs. For example, pressing one button could turn on the lights and adjust the temperature, while the other could start playing music or activate a security system.

The beauty of the Flick Duo lies in its ability to streamline control over a wide array of smart devices. Instead of fumbling through apps or voice commands, users can achieve multiple actions with a single, intuitive press. This kind of device is an excellent example of how smart home technology is evolving to be more user-friendly and efficient. The Flick Duo is just one of many devices that demonstrate the growing trend of simplifying smart home automation, making it accessible and enjoyable for everyone.

AI systems and voice assistants, like Amazon's Alexa, Google Assistant, and Apple's Siri, have become key players in the smart home ecosystem. These systems are revolutionizing how we interact with our homes by allowing voice control over everything from lights and appliances to entertainment systems and security cameras. With the ability to understand natural language commands and adapt to user preferences, these AI assistants make home automation effortless. They can set alarms, provide weather updates, and even offer reminders, all without requiring the user to lift a finger.

As more devices become interconnected through the Internet of Things (IoT), the possibilities for smart home automation continue to expand. Today, your home can learn your preferences and adjust the environment accordingly, whether it's adjusting the temperature, dimming the lights, or preparing your favorite playlist. The future of smart homes is one where technology anticipates our needs and responds intuitively to our commands, making our living spaces more comfortable, secure, and efficient.

In conclusion, gadgets like the Mudra Wristband, RayNeo Air 3S, Irvine AI-powered Doorbell, and Flick Duo Smart Button represent just a few of the many innovations shaping tomorrow's world. Wearable tech and smart home devices are paving the way for a more seamless, connected future, where our gadgets don't just serve us, they adapt to our lives, enhancing convenience, security, and entertainment in ways that were once unimaginable. As these technologies continue to evolve, they will undoubtedly redefine the way we interact with the world around us.

Chapter 3: Next-Generation AI and Machine Learning

AI as the Backbone of Modern Innovation

Artificial Intelligence (AI) has evolved from a futuristic concept to an essential driver of innovation, seamlessly integrating into almost every aspect of our daily lives. In today's tech landscape, AI is no longer confined to complex algorithms or research labs, it's embedded in consumer gadgets, gaming devices, cameras, and even everyday tools, acting as the backbone of modern technological advancement. From enhancing user experiences to automating tasks, AI powers a wide range of devices that are reshaping how we interact with the world.

Take, for instance, the AI-powered Ray-Ban Meta Glasses. These smart glasses are a perfect example of how AI is being woven into the fabric of personal technology. Equipped with a 12MP camera and AI functionalities, the Ray-Ban Meta Glasses allow users to capture images, record videos, make calls, and even stream live content, all from a stylish, hands-free device. The glasses use AI for real-time image recognition, which can identify objects, people, and even text, helping users interact with their surroundings in new, innovative ways.

Moreover, these glasses can also translate foreign languages on the fly, making them an indispensable tool for travelers or anyone looking to break down language barriers. With built-in voice control, users can ask questions, control media playback, or even get directions without ever lifting a finger. The incorporation of AI in such a device makes it not just a wearable tech gadget but a smart assistant in your pocket, elevating your experience and seamlessly integrating into your everyday routine.

Similarly, AI is transforming how we interact with gaming devices. AI-powered features in gaming consoles and accessories are revolutionizing gameplay, offering highly responsive environments that adapt to players' actions. From enhancing NPC behavior to adjusting in-game scenarios based on user input, AI is making video games more immersive and dynamic than ever before. AI doesn't just serve as an enhancement in gaming, it's fundamentally changing how games are designed, making them more interactive and lifelike.

In photography, AI-driven cameras have become the norm, as seen in devices like the Xiaomi 15 Ultra, with its 200MP camera and AI Ultra Zoom capabilities. This advanced AI technology optimizes images, recognizes scenes in real-time, and adjusts settings for the best possible shot. AI also powers features like portrait mode, where the device intelligently blurs the background to highlight the subject. It's clear that AI is playing a pivotal role in modern tech, and its reach extends across multiple industries, from entertainment and communication to security and healthcare.

The Role of Deep Learning in Personal Tech

At the heart of many modern AI systems lies deep learning, a branch of machine learning that uses neural networks to mimic the human brain's processing capabilities. Deep learning is responsible for much of the remarkable advancements in personal technology, powering devices that are more intelligent, intuitive, and capable of understanding complex inputs.

One standout example is the Mudra Wristband, a wearable that leverages deep learning to interpret neural signals for gesture recognition. The wristband's AI-driven deep learning algorithms read the electrical signals in the user's hand muscles and translate them into commands that control various devices. As the user interacts with the wristband, the deep learning system adapts, becoming more accurate over time and learning the user's gestures and preferences. This kind of personalized learning is central to the future of AI and showcases how deep learning can create highly specialized, user-friendly experiences.

Deep learning is also responsible for the intuitive behavior of smart assistants like Siri, Alexa, and Google Assistant. These virtual assistants have become much more than simple voice-activated tools, they've evolved into intelligent systems capable of understanding natural language, anticipating user needs, and learning from past interactions. Through continuous learning and real-time processing, smart assistants are becoming increasingly adept at predicting what we need before we even ask for it.

For example, if you've consistently asked your smart assistant to play a particular playlist every morning, it might start suggesting that playlist automatically when it detects you're starting your day. Over time, these assistants can learn your schedule, preferences, and even your tone of voice, enabling a more personalized experience that's incredibly efficient and intuitive.

This level of personalization, powered by deep learning, is transforming not only smart assistants but also entire ecosystems of connected devices. The more these devices interact with their users, the smarter they become. It's a cycle of continuous learning that allows technology to adapt and enhance itself based on the unique behaviors of each individual.

Smart Assistants: How They're Becoming More Intelligent and Intuitive

The rise of smart assistants has been one of the most transformative aspects of AI integration in personal tech. These AI-powered assistants are no longer just simple tools for performing basic tasks, they're evolving into highly intelligent systems capable of handling more complex requests and tasks.

At the heart of this evolution is natural language processing (NLP), which enables devices to understand human speech and interpret commands in a more human-like way. Smart assistants powered by advanced NLP can now understand context, respond to follow-up questions, and hold ongoing conversations. For example, if you ask Alexa about the weather, you can follow up with a question like, "What will the weather be like tomorrow?" and the assistant will understand that you're referring to the next day, not the current one.

The ability of smart assistants to "learn" is another key factor driving their intelligence. Through machine learning, these systems analyze data from millions of interactions, continually improving their ability to understand a wide variety of accents, dialects, and speech patterns. This allows them to interact with users in a way that feels increasingly natural and fluid.

Beyond just responding to voice commands, modern smart assistants are integrating with a growing number of IoT devices, offering seamless control over smart homes. Whether it's adjusting the thermostat, turning off lights, or starting your morning coffee, these assistants are becoming an integral part of daily life. As AI continues to improve, it's likely that smart assistants will become even more embedded in our routines, offering personalized, context-aware interactions that help us stay productive, informed, and entertained.

In the future, we might see even more advanced features, such as the ability for smart assistants to predict your needs before you ask or help guide you through complex tasks like cooking, home repairs, or even making decisions. The possibilities are vast, and as AI and deep learning continue to develop, we can only imagine how these systems will evolve.

In conclusion, AI and machine learning are no longer abstract concepts, they're the driving forces behind the next generation of personal technology. From the intelligent capabilities of the Mudra Wristband and Ray-Ban Meta Glasses to the deep learning algorithms that power smart assistants, AI is transforming how we live, work, and interact with the world. As these technologies continue to evolve, we're entering a future where AI will be even more ingrained in our daily lives, making our interactions with devices smarter, more personalized, and more intuitive than ever before. The journey of AI is just beginning, and the impact it will have on our world is only set to grow.

Chapter 4: Innovations in Photography and Imaging

The Future of Photography

Photography has come a long way since its humble beginnings, where capturing an image meant exposing film to light for a set period. Today, photography is not just an art form, but an intricate fusion of technology and creativity. With the rise of smartphones, digital cameras, and AI integration, the future of photography is rapidly shifting toward more versatile, intelligent, and immersive experiences. Gone are the days of bulky cameras with limited functionality, today's innovations are breaking the mold, offering powerful tools for both amateur photographers and professionals alike.

One of the key innovations in photography is the rise of modular camera systems. These systems offer flexibility that traditional cameras simply can't match. Take, for instance, the modular camera prototype, which attaches magnetically to smartphones to enhance their photographic capabilities. This device allows users to snap high-quality images, make zoom adjustments, and control focus with ease. The modular camera system is a game-changer in personal tech, as it combines the portability and convenience of smartphones with the high-level performance of professional-grade cameras. It's a perfect example of how technology is evolving to meet the demands of users who want the best of both worlds: the ease of use of a smartphone and the advanced features of a dedicated camera.

These modular systems also allow for the integration of a range of lenses and accessories that can be swapped out depending on the type of photography being pursued. Whether it's wide-angle shots, macro photography, or high-zoom telephoto images, the modular approach provides an unparalleled level of customization. The development of these systems speaks to a broader trend in tech: the pursuit of personalization and adaptability. People want gadgets that cater to their specific needs and preferences, and modular systems represent the future of customizable, high-performance photography tools.

The integration of AI into cameras has also revolutionized the way we capture images. AI algorithms now analyze a scene, adjust settings in real-time, and even enhance the quality of images, ensuring that the final product is as perfect as possible. Features like scene recognition, automatic exposure control, and AI-enhanced post-processing have made it easier than ever to take high-quality photos, even for those without a professional background. Whether you're snapping a portrait, a landscape, or an action shot, AI is there to assist, making subtle adjustments to ensure the best possible result every time.

The Role of 4K and Beyond in Visual Content

As cameras evolve, so too does the quality of visual content. The demand for higher-definition video and images has led to the widespread adoption of 4K resolution, and we're now pushing into even more advanced formats. 4K has become the standard for most modern devices, offering crisp, sharp visuals that were once unimaginable on consumer gadgets. From movies to video conferencing, the ability to record and display 4K content has changed the way we consume and create media.

4K cameras and devices have found their place in both consumer and professional environments. With the integration of AI, the quality of 4K visuals can now be optimized in real-time, resulting in a smoother and more vibrant viewing experience. The rise of 4K also has implications for fields like virtual reality (VR) and augmented reality (AR), where high-resolution visuals are essential for creating immersive experiences.

But 4K is just the beginning. As technology advances, we are moving toward 8K and even 16K content. These resolutions promise unimaginable levels of detail, paving the way for even more immersive and lifelike visual experiences. Whether it's streaming content on the latest smart TVs or capturing a moment with a next-generation smartphone camera, the pursuit of ever-higher resolution is pushing the boundaries of what we thought was possible.

The next leap in imaging technology lies in making these high-definition visuals more accessible and more portable. Devices like foldable projectors are emerging as an innovative solution to take 4K and beyond into the world of portable, immersive experiences. These compact, portable projectors allow users to display high-quality video and images anywhere, transforming any surface into a screen. The Arzen Zip Trifold Projector, for instance, is a foldable, portable 4K projector designed for on-the-go viewing. It's a perfect example of how visual content is not just about quality, it's about accessibility and convenience. With such devices, users can create their own cinema experience, transforming any space into a personal viewing area, whether it's for gaming, movies, or presentations.

Evolution of Camera Phones like the Xiaomi 15 Ultra

The development of camera phones is another prime example of how innovation in photography is driven by the desire for convenience and quality. Modern smartphones are equipped with advanced cameras that rival traditional point-and-shoot cameras and even DSLR devices. The Xiaomi 15 Ultra is a standout example, offering a 200MP camera, AI-powered zoom, and an ultra-large battery to support all of these powerful features.

What sets the Xiaomi 15 Ultra apart from its predecessors is its AI Ultra Zoom technology, which allows users to capture images with incredible detail and clarity from great distances. This feature is enhanced by AI, which adjusts the focus and exposure to ensure that the zoomed-in image is as sharp and vibrant as possible. Whether you're photographing a distant landscape or capturing fast-moving objects, the AI-powered zoom offers unparalleled quality, even in challenging conditions.

The smartphone's camera is also capable of recording in 8K, offering a level of video quality that was previously reserved for high-end professional equipment. The integration of AI further enhances the video-recording experience, optimizing the image and sound in real-time to produce the best possible results.

What's particularly exciting about the Xiaomi 15 Ultra and other smartphones following suit is how these devices have redefined what it means to be a camera phone. These aren't just tools for taking snapshots; they're powerful, multi-functional devices capable of handling a wide variety of professional-level imaging tasks. With AI integration, camera phones have evolved into more than just convenience devices, they've become essential tools for creators, influencers, journalists, and content producers across the globe.

As technology continues to improve, we can expect even more advanced camera systems to emerge, offering features like 3D imaging, real-time editing, and even AI-driven content creation. The line between professional cameras and smartphones is blurring, and the future of mobile photography looks incredibly bright.

In conclusion, the world of photography and imaging is undergoing a profound transformation, thanks to innovations like modular camera systems, AI-driven features, and the ongoing pursuit of higher-definition content. From the portability of modular systems to the breathtaking visuals made possible by 4K and beyond, the tools available today are empowering both casual users and professionals to capture and share the world in new, exciting ways. As AI continues to play a central role in the evolution of imaging technology, it's clear that the future of photography will be defined by ever-more intelligent, personalized, and immersive experiences.

Chapter 5: Wearable Tech and Augmented Reality (AR)

Exploring the Rise of AR and Wearable Devices

In the fast-paced world of technology, wearable devices have quickly become one of the most exciting and transformative categories of products. With advancements in artificial intelligence, sensors, and miniaturization, wearables are no longer just fitness trackers or smartwatches, they're becoming powerful extensions of ourselves, shaping the way we interact with both the digital and physical worlds. The integration of augmented reality (AR) into these wearables has brought about an entirely new dimension to human interaction with technology.

One of the most groundbreaking advancements in this space is the rise of AR glasses, which overlay digital content onto the real world. The RayNeo Air 3S is a prime example of how AR technology is evolving. These glasses offer an immersive experience, allowing users to view a 201-inch screen in their line of sight. They provide a 120Hz refresh rate, ensuring smooth and fluid visual experiences, whether for gaming, watching movies, or using apps. The lightweight design of the RayNeo Air 3S also makes them highly portable, unlike traditional AR headsets that often require cumbersome setups or tethering to a device.

The impact of AR glasses like the RayNeo Air 3S extends far beyond entertainment. They offer the potential for transforming how we work, communicate, and socialize. Imagine having an interactive display right in front of your eyes while attending a virtual meeting, or being able to navigate a foreign city with real-time translations and directions without ever pulling out your phone. AR glasses are not just a luxury, they're a tool that can enhance productivity, streamline communication, and enrich personal experiences. As we move towards a more connected world, these devices are poised to redefine how we interact with our environments, both digitally and physically.

In gaming, the potential of AR glasses is immense. They promise to bring virtual elements into the real world, offering experiences that blend the physical and digital in ways that were previously impossible. For example, imagine playing a game where the characters and objects exist around you in your living room, reacting to the physical space and even interacting with the environment in real-time. This level of immersion is not far off, and it's the type of experience that wearable AR devices like the RayNeo Air 3S aim to deliver.

Potential Use Cases in Gaming, Work, and Social Interaction

As the capabilities of AR glasses evolve, their potential applications will extend across a wide range of industries and sectors. In gaming, AR devices will enable immersive experiences that go far beyond the traditional screen. Gamers will be able to interact with characters and environments as if they were real, all while blending seamlessly with the real world. The ability to have 3D holograms and interactive objects floating in the room will revolutionize gaming as we know it. The lines between physical and virtual spaces will blur, providing players with a level of immersion previously reserved for sci-fi movies.

In the workplace, AR glasses offer a multitude of possibilities. For example, professionals in fields like architecture, engineering, and design can use AR to overlay 3D models and blueprints directly onto physical spaces, allowing for more efficient collaboration and real-time adjustments. Surgeons could use AR glasses to access important data during procedures, improving precision and reducing the risk of errors. The potential for AR in productivity is enormous, with glasses enabling workers to multitask more effectively, access information hands-free, and collaborate remotely with greater ease.

Social interaction is another area that will be greatly impacted by AR wearables. Imagine attending a concert and being able to see real-time subtitles for song lyrics or hearing live translations during an international event. AR glasses can also facilitate social interactions by providing real-time information about the people you meet, such as their names, interests, and shared connections. This ability to enhance face-to-face interaction with digital information will change the way we engage with others, making conversations more informative and connected. Social media apps could also find new ways to integrate AR, allowing users to interact with content in more dynamic ways, think of seeing your friends' posts float in front of you as you walk down the street or seeing interactive advertisements tailored to your preferences.

Another exciting aspect of AR glasses is the potential for social gaming. With the RayNeo Air 3S and similar devices, multiple users could join in on the same AR experience, interacting with the same virtual objects and environments in real time. This could transform not only the way we play games but also how we socialize and communicate online. The ability to share immersive experiences in real-time will open up new opportunities for collaboration, competition, and interaction.

The Future of Mixed Reality and Its Applications

The convergence of virtual reality (VR) and augmented reality (AR) has led to the development of mixed reality (MR), a space where the digital and physical worlds blend seamlessly together. Mixed reality allows users to interact with and manipulate both virtual objects and real-world environments simultaneously, creating an experience that is more immersive and dynamic than either VR or AR alone.

Wearable devices like AR glasses and smartwatches are key to the future of mixed reality. These devices will enable users to interact with their digital environments as if they were physically present within them. Imagine putting on a pair of AR glasses and stepping into a virtual world where the boundaries between the digital and physical dissolve. You could explore far-off places, interact with digital objects, or play games that require real-world movements, all while maintaining a connection to the environment around you.

One of the most significant potential applications of mixed reality is in education and training. MR could revolutionize how students and professionals learn, providing interactive, hands-on experiences that would otherwise be impossible. Medical students could practice surgeries in a simulated environment, architects could walk through their designs before they are built, and engineers could troubleshoot complex systems in real-time. The ability to simulate real-world environments and interact with them in meaningful ways will transform the way we approach education and skills development.

As mixed reality continues to evolve, the devices that support it will become more intuitive and sophisticated. We can expect future wearable devices to be lighter, more comfortable, and capable of processing complex data in real-time, making MR experiences more accessible and enjoyable. These advancements will open up new possibilities in entertainment, business, healthcare, and beyond.

Wearables like smartwatches and AR glasses will also play a crucial role in creating a more interconnected world. These devices will serve as bridges between the physical and digital realms, allowing us to navigate our environment with greater ease, while also staying connected to the digital world. For example, smartwatches may evolve to become more integrated with AR, allowing users to interact with both virtual elements and real-world data directly from their wrist. Similarly, AR glasses will become more streamlined and feature-rich, offering a wider range of functionalities for personal and professional use.

In conclusion, the rise of wearable technology and augmented reality is paving the way for a future where the lines between the physical and digital worlds blur. AR glasses, smartwatches, and other wearables are transforming how we interact with technology, enhancing both our personal and professional lives. As these devices continue to evolve, we can expect them to become more sophisticated, enabling a new era of mixed reality experiences that will change how we work, play, and communicate. The future of wearables and AR is incredibly exciting, and as technology advances, we're only scratching the surface of what's possible.

Chapter 6: The Power of Smart Laptops and Computers

Transforming the Computing Experience

In a world where technology is evolving at breakneck speeds, the personal computer remains one of the most essential tools in our daily lives. However, the traditional notion of a desktop or laptop has begun to shift, with newer innovations offering more dynamic, flexible, and efficient computing experiences. One of the most notable advancements in this space is the rise of foldable and multi-functional laptops, which have drastically altered how we use computers in both personal and professional settings.

Take, for instance, the Lenovo Flip Laptop. With its groundbreaking foldable OLED screen, this device is a perfect example of how versatility is being incorporated into modern laptops. Imagine a laptop that can transform from a traditional clamshell design into a tablet or even a fully extended flat screen. The Lenovo Flip Laptop's foldable OLED screen allows for just that, providing users with multiple modes to work, play, and consume content. Whether you're editing documents in laptop mode or streaming a movie in tablet mode, the flexibility offered by the Lenovo Flip allows for an entirely new level of multitasking. This design not only enhances productivity but also adds a layer of convenience that traditional laptops can't match.

This shift in laptop design is part of a larger trend of hybrid devices that combine the best features of various technologies, making them more adaptable to the user's needs. The ability to switch between different modes allows for smoother transitions between tasks, especially for professionals who may need to present on the go or work in environments where space is limited. Moreover, the use of OLED screens in foldable laptops brings vibrant color and sharp contrast to the user experience, improving everything from everyday productivity tasks to creative work like graphic design or video editing.

Another device making waves in the computing world is the ThinkBook 16P. Known for its attachable displays, this laptop pushes the boundaries of what we expect from a portable device. With the ability to expand your screen real estate through additional monitors, the ThinkBook 16P becomes a powerful tool for anyone needing more than a single display to enhance their work. Whether you're working on multiple documents simultaneously, editing videos, or managing complex data, the ability to add extra screens boosts productivity, reduces friction in multitasking, and allows for a more streamlined workflow. This flexibility opens new possibilities for professionals in fields like finance, design, and software development, where screen space and multitasking capabilities are critical to success.

Both the Lenovo Flip and the ThinkBook 16P represent a new frontier in personal computing, emphasizing versatility, multitasking, and user-centered design. These laptops are not just tools, they are dynamic platforms that adapt to the user's needs, making them indispensable for modern professionals and creatives alike.

The Role of Solar-Powered Tech

As we continue to innovate and push the boundaries of computing, sustainability has become a key consideration in tech design. The environmental impact of our devices, particularly when it comes to energy consumption, is something that the tech industry can no longer ignore. In response to this, solar-powered technology is emerging as one of the most exciting and practical solutions for improving the sustainability of laptops and other devices.

One of the most notable solar-powered devices in the market today is the Yoga Solar PC, a laptop that incorporates solar energy to extend battery life and reduce the reliance on traditional charging methods. The Yoga Solar PC is equipped with photovoltaic panels that absorb sunlight, converting it into energy to charge the battery. This means that the laptop can be charged even when you're on the go, without needing to plug into an electrical outlet. While solar charging may not yet be able to replace conventional charging entirely, it serves as a valuable supplement, especially for people who are often on the move or in locations where power outlets may not be readily available.

The Yoga Solar PC is an excellent example of how renewable energy can be integrated into personal tech to promote sustainability without compromising performance. As energy consumption continues to grow worldwide, the demand for more efficient and environmentally friendly devices will increase, and the Yoga Solar PC represents a promising step forward. By using solar power, users can not only extend the life of their device but also contribute to a more sustainable and eco-friendly future.

The impact of solar-powered tech goes beyond just the convenience of having a backup power source, it also speaks to a larger shift in the tech industry towards more responsible and sustainable product development. In a world where e-waste is a growing problem, innovations like solar-powered laptops represent a future where tech devices are designed with both performance and the environment in mind. As solar energy technology improves and becomes more affordable, we can expect to see even more devices adopting this model, reducing the overall carbon footprint of our gadgets and empowering users to make eco-conscious choices without sacrificing convenience or power.

Looking ahead, it's clear that the future of personal computing will not only be shaped by new performance enhancements and features but also by an increased focus on sustainability. With the advent of solar-powered laptops and the broader adoption of renewable energy in tech products, we can look forward to a future where our devices are not only smarter but also more environmentally friendly. The Yoga Solar PC is just the beginning, and as solar technology continues to advance, it's exciting to imagine a future where our devices can charge themselves with nothing more than the power of the sun.

Conclusion

The power of smart laptops and computers lies in their ability to adapt to the evolving needs of users, providing a combination of performance, flexibility, and sustainability. Devices like the Lenovo Flip Laptop and the ThinkBook 16P demonstrate how modern technology is reimagining what it means to be productive in a digital world. These devices go beyond the traditional notion of a laptop, they offer new possibilities for multitasking, collaboration, and creativity.

At the same time, the emergence of solar-powered technology, exemplified by the Yoga Solar PC, shows how the tech industry is beginning to incorporate renewable energy solutions to reduce its environmental impact. As technology continues to evolve, we can expect to see even more advancements that combine performance with sustainability, creating a future where our devices not only improve our lives but also help protect the planet.

In this chapter, we've seen how smart laptops and computers are redefining the computing experience, pushing the boundaries of what's possible with foldable screens, attachable displays, and solar-powered energy solutions. As we move further into the future, these innovations will continue to shape how we interact with technology, making it more versatile, sustainable, and integral to our everyday lives.

Chapter 7: Gaming Innovations: Next-Level Experiences

Revolutionizing Gaming Hardware

The gaming world has always been at the forefront of technological progress, acting as both a testing ground and showcase for cutting-edge innovation. In recent years, advancements in gaming hardware have gone beyond faster processors and better graphics, they now encompass devices that merge comfort, accessibility, and performance in unprecedented ways. One such breakthrough is the Project Ariel Gaming Chair, a piece of equipment that has redefined what it means to immerse oneself in a game. This isn't just a chair, it's an intelligent gaming station designed to respond to every movement and action with real-time feedback. From haptic vibrations that simulate in-game actions to an ergonomic design that supports long hours of play, the Project Ariel chair provides a full-body experience that draws the player deeper into virtual environments. It blurs the lines between the physical and digital, turning a passive seating arrangement into an active part of the gaming journey.

Just as significant is the rise of devices that elevate mobile gaming. The OAP Mcom Smartphone Gaming Controller exemplifies how smartphones are being transformed into powerful gaming consoles. With its ergonomic design, responsive buttons, and precision control sticks, this device connects seamlessly to a smartphone, offering the kind of tactile experience once exclusive to traditional consoles. It provides players with console-grade control on the go, effectively bridging the gap between casual gaming and competitive play. As mobile games grow more complex and graphically intensive, the need for controllers like the OAP Mcom becomes even more apparent, especially for gamers who crave accuracy and speed during gameplay. It's no longer just about swiping and tapping, a real controller adds the nuance and control necessary for high-level performance.

These innovations demonstrate how gaming hardware is being designed with the user in mind, focusing not just on raw power but on how gamers interact with and experience their games. Comfort, immersion, and flexibility are no longer luxuries, they're expectations in a gaming landscape that values both casual fun and intense competition. Whether on a console, PC, or smartphone, the goal is the same: to create a seamless connection between player and game, and new hardware is making that vision a reality.

Immersive Gaming with AR Glasses and Controllers

As exciting as hardware upgrades are, the real transformation in gaming is happening with augmented reality (AR). This isn't a trend or gimmick, it's a seismic shift in how we engage with virtual environments. Wearable devices like AR glasses are redefining the boundaries of gaming realism, offering a hybrid world where digital objects overlay the physical, creating a fusion of imagination and reality. No longer confined to screens, games can now unfold in the space around the player, bringing a new dimension to interactivity.

Imagine wearing lightweight AR glasses and seeing game elements appear on your coffee table or living room wall. That's the kind of experience RayNeo Air 3S and similar devices are delivering. These AR glasses allow players to step into mixed-reality environments where they're not just controlling a character, they're part of the world. Whether it's battling monsters that appear in your backyard or solving puzzles projected onto your kitchen counter, the lines between game and reality are beginning to dissolve. The experience becomes deeply personal and physical, drawing players into an immersive narrative that reacts to their surroundings and movements.

Complementing AR glasses are new-gen motion and gesture controllers that further enhance gameplay. These devices track hand movements with precision, enabling players to interact with digital environments naturally. Instead of pressing buttons, you can swing a sword, cast a spell, or navigate a menu with just a flick of your wrist. This kind of intuitive control adds a layer of realism that traditional gaming setups simply can't replicate. It's not just about seeing a game differently, it's about playing it differently, engaging both the body and the mind.

Together, AR glasses and wearable controllers are transforming gaming into a multisensory experience. This combination offers freedom of movement, intuitive interaction, and deeply immersive gameplay that feels more like living a story than playing one. The implications stretch far beyond entertainment, too these technologies are being explored for training simulations, fitness games, and educational experiences, blurring the boundaries between gaming and real-world applications.

The future of gaming lies in the ability to step beyond the screen, and thanks to innovations in hardware and AR integration, that future is already arriving. As these devices become more affordable and widely available, the gaming experience will continue to evolve into something far more dynamic, inclusive, and immersive than ever before.

Chapter 8: Sustainability and the Future of Tech

The Role of Green Tech in Tomorrow's Gadgets

The intersection of technology and sustainability has emerged as one of the most compelling shifts in modern innovation. As the demand for smart devices continues to rise, so does the urgency to make them more eco-friendly. The focus is no longer solely on what gadgets can do, but also on how they do it—quietly shaping a future where performance and responsibility coexist. Among the standout developments is the rise of solar-powered technology, offering a cleaner, renewable approach to powering our digital lives. The Yoga Solar PC is a shining example of this progress, integrating solar energy harvesting into its sleek design to reduce dependence on traditional charging methods. This not only enhances energy efficiency but also extends usability in remote or off-grid environments. It transforms the everyday laptop into a symbol of conscious consumption, merging innovation with environmental stewardship.

Equally impressive is the work being done by Dryad Networks, whose solar-powered sensors are redefining environmental monitoring. Their Wildfire Detection system uses mesh networking and solar technology to provide early alerts for wildfires, saving ecosystems, lives, and property. These devices are designed to operate independently in forested areas without requiring external power sources, showing how green tech can serve both high-tech efficiency and critical ecological needs. In this way, sustainability is not a side project, it's at the very core of life-saving innovation.

Another critical area of development is in portable, renewable energy sources that empower users to stay connected without relying on the grid. The Cow P1 Off-the-Grid Power Supply stands out in this category, offering a rugged and reliable solution for anyone needing energy independence. Designed for campers, travelers, emergency responders, and people living in areas with unreliable electricity, this device stores enough power to charge smartphones, laptops, and small appliances. Its portability and compatibility with solar panels make it a practical answer to the growing need for energy on the go, without leaving a carbon footprint. It's a step toward a future where everyone has access to clean energy wherever they are, reinforcing the idea that personal freedom and sustainability can go hand in hand.

These innovations are not just about convenience, they reflect a shift in the tech industry's mindset. The emphasis on renewable energy and sustainable functionality signals a broader recognition of technology's responsibility in addressing climate change. As demand grows for longer-lasting, self-sufficient devices, solar integration and off-grid power are becoming essential components of design rather than futuristic novelties.

How Tech Can Reduce Environmental Impact

Beyond individual gadgets, a deeper movement is taking place, one that rethinks the very materials and methods used to build modern technology. Sustainable design practices are becoming an industry standard, pushing manufacturers to reconsider everything from packaging to product lifespan. Companies are exploring biodegradable materials, recyclable components, and modular designs that allow users to upgrade parts rather than discard entire devices. This modularity not only reduces waste but also encourages a more intentional relationship between consumers and their gadgets.

One promising approach is the use of recycled metals and plastics in production, which not only cuts down on environmental degradation but also decreases reliance on mining operations that are often resource-intensive and environmentally harmful. Tech giants and startups alike are beginning to prioritize supply chain transparency and eco-friendly sourcing, signaling a shift in both ethics and efficiency.

The integration of renewable energy into consumer electronics also plays a critical role. By enabling devices to charge via solar panels or kinetic energy, companies are reducing the strain on traditional power grids and lowering the overall carbon output associated with everyday device use. Smart power management features, such as automatic sleep modes, energy-efficient processors, and low-power displays are now standard in many modern devices, showing that even small adjustments can collectively make a significant environmental impact.

Furthermore, digital transformation in industries like transportation, agriculture, and manufacturing is leading to better energy monitoring, smarter resource use, and lower emissions overall. Technologies like AI-driven logistics systems reduce fuel consumption, while precision farming powered by smart sensors conserves water and soil quality. Even in the realm of software, energy-efficient algorithms and cloud services are being optimized to run on greener data centers.

In the long run, sustainable tech is more than a trend, it's a necessity. As the planet faces escalating environmental challenges, the responsibility of the tech industry has never been greater. The future will favor devices and systems that don't just perform well, but also contribute positively to the ecosystem. The next era of gadgets won't just be smart, they'll be sustainable, forming the backbone of a world where innovation serves both people and the planet.

Chapter 9: Health and Wellbeing: Gadgets for a Better Life

Tech for Monitoring and Improving Health

The intersection of health and technology is revolutionizing how individuals approach personal wellness, making proactive care more accessible, intuitive, and integrated into everyday life. Devices are no longer just tools, they're companions that monitor, advise, and even predict health needs with striking precision. One of the most groundbreaking innovations in this space is the Beo Home Health Monitor. Designed for home use, it enables users to conduct medical-grade diagnostics without visiting a clinic. With built-in sensors and AI-driven analysis, it captures vital health data such as blood pressure, oxygen levels, heart rate, and other critical indicators. This empowers users with real-time insights into their well-being and allows for early detection of potential health issues, transforming passive observation into active prevention.

Wearable technology has also become a vital part of this health revolution. Smartwatches and fitness bands now come equipped with sensors capable of tracking heart rate variability, blood oxygen saturation, stress levels, and even irregular heart rhythms. These features are particularly valuable for people managing chronic conditions, as they allow continuous tracking and easy data sharing with healthcare providers. Real-time updates help users adjust their lifestyle choices, whether it's sleep quality, hydration, or daily movement, giving them greater control over their bodies and habits. Instead of health being something managed in the doctor's office, it becomes an ongoing dialogue facilitated by tech.

This hands-on approach to personal health is fostering a culture where awareness and accountability are no longer intimidating but empowering. It's a major shift from a reactive healthcare system to one that prioritizes prevention, personalization, and engagement. Users are no longer waiting for symptoms to appear, they're leveraging tech to stay one step ahead, building a healthier lifestyle from the ground up with digital support systems.

The Future of Mental Health and Wellness Tech

Beyond physical wellness, mental health has become a crucial focal point in the evolution of health technology. The stresses of modern life from digital overload to work-life imbalance have made anxiety, burnout, and sleep disorders more common than ever. In response, tech innovators are designing gadgets that promote relaxation, mindfulness, and emotional balance. Among them, the Ver Leaf Prime stands out for its simplicity and effectiveness. This device helps users lower stress and improve sleep by using guided breathing exercises, calming light therapy, and biofeedback. It doesn't just suggest relaxation, it facilitates it, giving users a tangible way to manage mental wellness from their bedside table or work desk.

The value of such devices lies in their accessibility. Not everyone has the time or resources to attend therapy sessions or wellness retreats, but most people can access a gadget that provides mental support on demand. These tools act as a first line of defense, offering immediate relief and consistent practice to manage emotional well-being. From sleep trackers that gently adjust your circadian rhythm to meditation aids that sync with your breathing, today's tech is becoming more attuned to the inner workings of the human mind.

Wearables also play a pivotal role in this space. Smart rings and watches now offer stress detection features that analyze physical cues like skin temperature, heart rate, and movement, to notify users when they may need a moment to decompress. Some even guide users through mindfulness sessions or suggest breathing exercises when stress is detected, helping them regain calm before emotions escalate. This seamless integration into daily routines helps normalize mental wellness as part of self-care, rather than an afterthought.

Tech companies are also exploring neurotechnology, devices that can influence or monitor brain activity through gentle electrical stimulation or EEG sensors. These tools are being tested to treat anxiety, depression, and attention disorders, offering promising alternatives to traditional medications. With time, such innovations could democratize mental health care, making it accessible at home, without stigma or institutional barriers.

The future of wellness lies in this blend of smart design, advanced sensors, and human-centric features. Gadgets are becoming more intuitive, less intrusive, and better aligned with the nuanced needs of their users. As health challenges grow more complex, technology is responding not with cold machinery, but with empathetic, thoughtful tools designed to uplift body and mind. The vision isn't just about curing illness, it's about nurturing well-being in a world that often forgets to pause, reflect, and breathe.

Chapter 10: The Future of Work and Productivity

How Tech is Transforming the Workplace

The modern workplace is undergoing a transformation unlike anything seen before, thanks to rapid advances in technology that redefine how, when, and where work gets done. As companies adapt to more flexible, decentralized operations, tools designed for productivity are stepping into the spotlight. At the center of this evolution are AI-powered productivity platforms and compact devices that bring full-scale computing into smaller, more adaptable forms. One notable innovation in this space is the Mecha Comment Mini Computer, a multifunctional device that combines portability, AI integration, and robust performance, giving professionals the power of a desktop setup in the palm of their hands. It's more than just a computer; it's a smart assistant, project manager, and creative tool all rolled into one.

These new technologies aren't just about doing more; they're about doing things differently. AI-driven apps and devices are reshaping tasks that once took hours into processes that are now streamlined and intelligent. Document editing, scheduling, data analysis, and even customer engagement are increasingly automated, freeing workers from mundane routines so they can focus on strategy and creativity. Video conferencing tools, virtual whiteboards, and cloud-based collaboration platforms now allow teams to work together from any corner of the globe with seamless efficiency. The remote work movement, once a necessity, has evolved into a lifestyle that prioritizes autonomy, balance, and tech-enabled productivity.

Tech also plays a crucial role in reducing cognitive overload. Smart assistants integrated into laptops, phones, and wearables offer timely reminders, optimize workflows, and help users stay on track with minimal effort. Noise-canceling headphones, ergonomic hardware, and virtual office environments are creating distraction-free zones even in the most chaotic settings. The shift isn't just physical, it's mental. Technology is helping people concentrate better, communicate clearer, and stay mentally aligned with their goals in an increasingly dynamic work environment.

The Rise of Modular and Customizable Tech for Professionals

As the demands of modern professionals become more varied, so too must the tools they use. Gone are the days of one-size-fits-all hardware; in their place is a new era of modular, customizable tech that adapts to different tasks, environments, and user preferences. Leading this charge is the ThinkBook 16P, especially when paired with Magic Bay's magnetic dual-screen system. This setup allows users to expand or reduce their display real estate based on their needs, whether they're working on a complex design project, managing spreadsheets, or running video calls and presentations simultaneously. The magnetic attachment system makes switching between configurations effortless, combining functionality with aesthetic appeal.

This trend toward modularity isn't just about convenience, it's about empowering users to build a workspace that aligns with their unique workflow. Professionals now expect more than just a fast processor or long battery life; they want tech that evolves with them, supports multitasking, and offers versatility on demand. Devices with detachable keyboards, adjustable stands, or foldable screens are becoming more mainstream as people seek seamless transitions between work, travel, and leisure. The ability to swap components, expand capabilities, and customize setups ensures longevity and relevance in a fast-moving tech landscape.

Furthermore, modular tech encourages sustainability. Instead of replacing entire devices, users can upgrade specific components, extending the life cycle of their tools and reducing e-waste. This shift aligns with the values of younger, eco-conscious professionals who prioritize efficiency without compromising the environment.

What's emerging is a world where technology doesn't just support productivity, it enhances it through smart design, adaptability, and personalization. Devices are no longer passive tools but active partners in the creative and professional journey. Whether it's through the intelligent power of the Mecha Comment Mini

Computer or the visual freedom of dual-screen laptops, the future of work is being crafted by tools that think, adapt, and grow alongside the people who use them.

Chapter 11: Transportation and Mobility

Tech Shaping the Future of Travel

Transportation is undergoing a radical transformation, and technology is at the wheel. As urban spaces grow denser and global connectivity becomes essential, mobility solutions are evolving to meet these demands. One of the most groundbreaking innovations is the development of autonomous vehicles. Self-driving cars, buses, and delivery systems are being designed not just to take people from point A to B, but to redefine the very nature of mobility. These vehicles are powered by complex AI systems and a suite of sensors that allow them to navigate, learn, and adapt to real-world environments with minimal human input. This evolution promises to reduce accidents, improve traffic flow, and provide mobility to those who otherwise might not have access.

Another major leap in future mobility is the hyperloop system, a high-speed, low-resistance transport method that uses magnetic levitation and vacuum tubes to transport pods at speeds faster than commercial airliners. The concept, once science fiction, is being tested and developed by tech giants and startups alike, with the goal of cutting long-distance travel down to minutes. The implications for global business, tourism, and logistics are massive. People could commute between cities hundreds of miles apart in under an hour, dramatically shifting where and how we live and work.

Tech is also influencing traditional transportation through smart mobility gadgets and systems. Navigation tools, real-time traffic analysis, ride-sharing platforms, and connected public transport infrastructure are making commutes smarter, more efficient, and more sustainable. Cities are integrating smart sensors into traffic lights, parking meters, and transport fleets to reduce congestion and optimize energy use. These interconnected systems are giving rise to the concept of smart cities, urban areas where mobility is seamless, data-driven, and eco-friendly.

Personal Transport Innovations

As transportation advances on a macro level, it's also evolving on a personal scale. Commuters and everyday travelers now have access to compact, powerful devices that make their journeys smoother and more convenient. The Airgo 2, a portable air pump, is a perfect example of how mobility tech is adapting to personal needs. Designed to be lightweight and travel-friendly, it allows cyclists, e-scooter users, and even drivers to inflate tires or sports gear anywhere, anytime. It reflects a broader movement toward on-the-go solutions that cater to modern lifestyles and the increasing popularity of personal electric transport.

Electric scooters, hoverboards, foldable bikes, and portable chargers are now essentials for many urban dwellers. These devices provide alternatives to traditional vehicles, allowing people to avoid traffic, reduce carbon emissions, and maintain flexibility in how they move around. Smart helmets with built-in communication systems, GPS, and lights add another layer of safety and functionality, while app-connected e-bikes can monitor health stats, battery levels, and route optimization in real-time.

The integration of AI and IoT into personal transport has also led to improvements in predictive maintenance, theft prevention, and navigation. Users can now receive alerts when a part is likely to fail or be reminded to recharge before their next journey. These small yet impactful upgrades are changing expectations around mobility and creating a more informed, empowered commuter.

Even in rural or off-grid areas, advancements in portable mobility tech are making an impact. Devices like compact solar-powered chargers, emergency communication gadgets, and modular backpacks with embedded power supplies are giving explorers and remote workers the freedom to travel further without losing connectivity or access to essential tools.

The future of transportation is no longer just about getting somewhere faster, it's about doing so smarter, safer, and more sustainably. From the rise of self-driving vehicles and high-speed transit systems to everyday gadgets like the Airgo 2, technology is expanding what's possible in both global travel and personal mobility. As innovation continues to push boundaries, the journey becomes just as transformative as the destination.

Chapter 12: Security and Privacy in a Connected World

Tech That Enhances Personal and Home Security

In today's hyper-connected world, personal and home security has evolved beyond locks and alarms. Technology is redefining how we protect ourselves, our data, and our environments. One of the most revolutionary innovations is Amazon One, a biometric authentication system that uses palm recognition to authorize payments and grant access. This contactless technology scans unique patterns of veins and ridges in a person's palm, making it not only more secure than traditional methods but also more convenient. It allows for seamless entry into locations or quick transactions without the need for physical cards or smartphones. As this kind of biometric tech gains popularity, the concept of identity verification is shifting from something we carry to something we are.

Smart security systems are becoming more intelligent and integrated than ever. AI-powered doorbells and surveillance cameras are no longer passive recording tools, they're active guardians. These devices can detect motion, recognize faces, differentiate between strangers and familiar visitors, and even alert homeowners in real-time with detailed notifications. Systems like Irvine's AI doorbell offer facial recognition and behavior tracking, enabling users to take immediate action through their connected devices, whether they're at home or thousands of miles away.

Advanced home security now includes smart locks, sensors, and connected lighting systems that simulate occupancy when you're away. These innovations not only deter potential intruders but also add layers of convenience, such as remotely unlocking doors for guests or delivery personnel. The interconnectedness of these devices, managed through centralized platforms or voice assistants, provides a new level of control and peace of mind that traditional security methods simply can't match.

The Balance Between Convenience and Privacy

While these technological advancements have significantly increased personal security, they've also sparked essential conversations around privacy. The more integrated our lives become with digital devices, the more data we generate and this data, when mishandled, can pose serious risks. Facial recognition, palm scans, and AI monitoring tools raise ethical questions about surveillance, data ownership, and the potential for misuse.

Many tech companies now have access to highly sensitive information, from our physical biometrics to our daily routines. While this data helps power the intelligent features we enjoy, such as personalized recommendations or proactive security alerts, it also opens the door to privacy infringements. For example, a smart assistant listening for commands can inadvertently capture conversations, and security footage stored on cloud servers may become vulnerable to breaches if not properly protected.

The trade-off between convenience and privacy is a growing concern. Users want seamless, intuitive technology, but not at the cost of their personal freedoms. As such, the demand for transparency, ethical data handling, and enhanced cybersecurity is higher than ever.

People are increasingly aware of the need to understand how their data is collected, stored, and used and they expect tech providers to take accountability.

To address these concerns, privacy-focused features are becoming more common. End-to-end encryption, two-factor authentication, local data storage options, and customizable privacy settings are being integrated into devices and platforms. These features empower users to control their information and choose the level of access granted to apps and services.

In this evolving landscape, the future of security and privacy hinges on balance. As tech continues to innovate, the challenge lies in building systems that are not only efficient and secure but also respectful of individual rights. Security should never come at the expense of privacy, and convenience should not overshadow the need for ethical responsibility.

Ultimately, the connected world brings both promise and responsibility. Innovations like Amazon One and AI-powered security tools are reshaping what safety looks like but with them comes a crucial obligation to safeguard our most personal information. As we move forward, this delicate balance will define how technology fits into our lives, and whether it truly serves to protect or control.

Chapter 13: The Road Ahead: What's Next for Tech?

Where We're Headed in the Next Decade

The rapid pace of technological advancement over the past few decades is only a preview of what the future holds. As we look ahead, the next ten years promise a surge of even more transformative innovations, devices and systems that will make today's cutting-edge tech feel basic by comparison. At the heart of this next wave are breakthroughs in artificial intelligence, augmented reality, and wearable technology, which are poised to become more immersive, intuitive, and integrated into our daily lives than ever before.

AI is expected to evolve far beyond task automation and into deeper contextual awareness. Personal assistants will anticipate needs without being asked, autonomous systems will learn from emotional cues, and devices will begin to understand not just what we want, but why we want it. These systems will become more empathetic, able to respond to human emotions, health indicators, and behavioral patterns to provide meaningful support in both personal and professional environments.

Augmented reality is also primed for a leap forward. Devices like the RayNeo Air 3S have laid the foundation for wearable displays, but in the coming years, AR will move from novelty to necessity. Glasses will become lighter, more fashionable, and seamlessly capable of blending virtual content with the real world, making them ideal tools for education, work collaboration, and social interaction. Cities may even begin to adapt with AR-friendly signage, navigation systems, and smart infrastructure that communicate directly with wearable tech.

Wearables themselves will continue expanding beyond fitness and communication. With advances in flexible electronics and nanotechnology, future wearables could be embedded in clothing, jewelry, or even under the skin, offering real-time health diagnostics, brain-computer interface control, or remote collaboration capabilities. These devices will redefine how we think about personal technology not just as tools, but as extensions of ourselves.

The Potential of Futuristic Tech to Solve Global Challenges

Beyond personal convenience and entertainment, the most powerful promise of emerging technologies lies in their ability to address global challenges. The integration of smart, sustainable tech is already reshaping how we tackle some of the world's most pressing issues, particularly environmental crises.

Take Dryad Networks' wildfire detection system, for example. Using a network of solar-powered sensors and AI-driven analytics, it can identify and report the earliest signs of a fire, often before smoke is visible to satellites or human observers. This kind of proactive environmental monitoring could become the blueprint for preventing large-scale disasters and minimizing the damage caused by climate change. As these systems scale, they could be used to detect floods, landslides, or air pollution, providing communities with vital time to respond and prepare.

Solar-powered technology as a whole is gaining traction, not only as a power source for emergency and remote devices, but also as a sustainable alternative for everyday consumer electronics. Gadgets like the Yoga Solar PC illustrate how we can reduce reliance on grid energy without sacrificing performance. In regions with limited access to electricity, solar tech can enable education, communication, and economic participation, bridging gaps that have long hindered development.

Moreover, smart agriculture tools, water conservation systems, and decentralized energy grids are being driven by innovations in AI and IoT. These solutions offer hope for more equitable resource distribution and resilience in the face of growing climate instability. In this vision of the future, tech doesn't just entertain or assist, it empowers communities, protects ecosystems, and reinforces sustainability.

Ultimately, the road ahead is not just about sleeker designs or faster processors, it's about relevance and responsibility. As we invent the tools of tomorrow, we must also consider the kind of future we're building with them. Every new gadget, every advancement in AI, every leap in connectivity carries the potential to either unite or divide, uplift or overlook.

What's clear is that technology will be inseparable from our everyday experience in the decade to come. But more than just living with it, we have the opportunity to live better because of it. Whether it's through smarter devices, immersive interfaces, or sustainable innovations, the next era of tech is set to define not only how we interact with the world but how we shape it.

Conclusion: Embracing the Tech Wave

Why These Innovations Matter

The world we live in today is the result of centuries of discovery, experimentation, and innovation, but the pace at which change is occurring now is unlike anything humanity has ever experienced. Technology is no longer something that exists on the periphery of our lives, it's at the very center, shaping the way we communicate, work, travel, heal, and connect. Embracing the wave of modern tech is not just about staying current with trends; it's about recognizing the immense potential these innovations carry to solve real-world problems and enhance the human experience.

From the smallest smartwatches to AI-powered glasses, modular laptops, and solar-powered systems, each innovation contributes to a broader ecosystem of progress. These gadgets don't just represent advancements in engineering, they reflect a shift in how we define convenience, productivity, and even sustainability. They allow us to live healthier lives by tracking vital health data in real time. They help us reduce our carbon footprint by utilizing renewable energy and improving energy efficiency. They empower us to work from anywhere, learn faster, and remain connected in ways we never thought possible.

Technology today also carries the promise of inclusion. It bridges geographical divides, breaks down barriers to education and healthcare, and provides new tools for communities that have long been underserved. The beauty of this ongoing tech wave lies in its scalability, what begins as luxury or novelty can quickly become a necessity that transforms lives across socioeconomic lines.

But these breakthroughs also bring with them a responsibility: to use them wisely. As our gadgets grow more intelligent and interconnected, we must be mindful of privacy, ethics, and sustainability. It's not enough to adopt new tech, we must ensure that our embrace of innovation is balanced with intention and foresight.

A Call to Action for Readers

The future isn't something that's coming, it's something we're already living in. Whether you're a tech enthusiast, a casual user, or someone just beginning to explore the digital world, now is the time to lean in. Stay curious. Stay informed. Ask questions and seek out knowledge about the tools and systems shaping tomorrow. Don't be afraid to experiment with new gadgets or dive into unfamiliar technologies. The more you understand the direction tech is taking, the more empowered you'll be to adapt, thrive, and lead within it.

This wave of innovation is relentless, but it's also filled with opportunity, for creativity, connection, and change. By embracing it with an open mind, we allow ourselves to become not just users of technology, but active participants in designing the future. Every decision we make about the tech we adopt, support, or create has a ripple effect that contributes to the world we're building.

So let this not be the end of the journey, but the beginning of a more engaged and intentional relationship with technology. Embrace the advancements. Explore the possibilities. And above all, remain open to the evolution, because the future isn't waiting, it's already here.